Day Trading

Day Trading: Beginners Guide to the Best Strategies, Tools, Tactics and Psychology to Profit from Outstanding Short-term Trading Opportunities on Stock Market, Futures, Cryptocurrencies and Forex

By

David Reese

Table of Contents

4

Introduction

Congratulations on downloading *Day Trading* and thank you for doing so.

The following chapters will discuss everything that you need to know to get started with day trading. Day trading is a great method that many traders may be hesitant about joining but as a beginner, it is a great way for you to enter the market and make a lot of money in a short amount of time. With day trading, you purchase a stock, hopefully at a low price, and then sell it during the same day at a higher price. If you can do this many times during the day, you can start to earn quite a bit of profit in the stock market.

This guidebook is going to take some time to explore day trading and how to get started with this process. It may seem intimidating in the beginning but we will go over some of the best strategies that you can use to really make it work for you. In addition to some of the top strategies for day trading, we will also look through the basics of day trading, how to pick out a good brokerage account, how to limit your risks a bit, and so much more.

Whether you have spent some time investing in the stock market or you are a beginner at all kinds of investing, this guidebook is the right choice for you. Make sure to take a look and learn all the tips and tricks and best strategies to make day trading work for you.

There are plenty of books on this subject on the market, so thanks again for choosing this one! Every effort was made to ensure it is full of as much useful information as possible. Please enjoy!

Chapter 1:
What Is Day Trading

There are many different options when it comes to entering the stock market. Some are long-term investments where you make an income each quarter on the stocks you purchase. Others, like day trading, will be short-term with the whole trade occurring in one day.

Day trading is the buying and selling of securities in one single trading day. This can occur in any type of marketplace that you choose but it is most common in the stock market and in the forex market. Typically, to do well as a day trader, you need to have some knowledge about your chosen market and you need to have money. A day trader is going to utilize high amounts of leverage with some short-term trading strategies in order to capitalize on the small price movements that happen in a very liquid stock.

Day trading is very fast paced. You will purchase a stock, bond, option or other security at some point during the day. Then, sometime during the same day, you will sell the security. If you watched the market properly and the trade goes well, you will make a profit from that sale. If you made a mistake with your calculations, you will lose money.

You do not want to let your trade go on to the next day. This requires a different type of strategy than you will use with day trading. Mixing strategies during the same trade just to avoid a loss will actually make things worse. It is better to cut your losses with that trade and move on, closing out the trade before the end of the day.

With day trading, you are not going to make a ton of money off each trade. In fact, if you make a few dollars with each trade, you are doing a good job. The point here is to do a lot of little trades, taking advantage of the temporary ups and downs of the market. A lot of little profits can add up to a good payday when the process is done.

The potential profit that you can make from day traded is often misunderstood on Wall Street. There are many internet scams that like to take on this confusion and capitalize on it making a ton of money by promising large returns in a short period of time. On the other side, the media continues to promote this trading method as a get rich quick scheme.

To determine whether you will be successful depends on a few important factors. Mainly, if you jump into the day trading game without enough knowledge about the market and how this trading method works, you will probably fail. But there are many day traders who are able to make a successful living from day trading. These individuals know about the market, have a good strategy in place, and can work with the market, despite the risks.

Day trading can be difficult. There are many professional financial advisors and money managers who worry about the risk of day trading and will shy away from it. They worry that in many cases, the reward is not going to justify all the risk that you take with day trading. It is possible to make a profit in this method but you have to really know the market and you must have the time to fully watch the market at all times while completing your trade. Even those who do well in day trading will admit that the success rate with this method is often lower than the other methods of stock market trading.

Common Characteristics of a Day Trader

Professional day traders are those who do this type of trading for a living. While other forms of trading can sometimes be done as a hobby or a gambling high, day trading is often not included here. Day traders are typically well-established in the field and they have spent quite a bit of time working in the stock market. This makes them equipped to recognize changes in the market and to learn the trends of various industries, helping them to pick out the right trades to make money with day trading. Some of the prerequisites to day trading include:

- Experience and some knowledge about the marketplace.

If you don't have a good understanding of the market and its fundamentals, you will most likely lose money.

- Enough money to start.
  You need to have some savings or other money that you can put towards day trading. Make sure this is money that you can afford to lose. This helps to keep some emotions out of the trade and can help you make smarter choices with your trades. Often, you will need a large amount of capital is needed to capitalize effectively in this type of trading.

- A good strategy.
  A trader needs to have a way to beat out the rest of the market. There are many strategies (some of which we will talk about later) that can help you with day trading. Each them can be effective; you just need to pick the one you feel comfortable with.

- Discipline.

All day traders need to have some discipline. If you aren't able to stick with your chosen strategy, then you will lose money. Success is virtually impossible without some discipline.

Using Day Trading to Make a Living

There are two divisions when it comes to professional day traders. The first one is those who work alone. The second is those who work for a larger company. Most traders who do this kind of trading for a living will work for a large company. This is helpful because these individuals will have access to a lot of tools that an individual trader only dreams about. These can include some expensive analytical software, a lot of leverage and capital to start, and a direct line to the trading desk. These types of traders are looking for profits that are easy and ones that can be made looking at news events and arbitrage opportunities.

This doesn't mean that an individual trader isn't able to do day trading on their own. They may not have a trading desk of their own but they may have some strong ties to a brokerage and some other resources. If you are an individual trader, you won't be able to compete with some of the larger companies, but there is still a niche market that you can join.

If you wish to use day trading as a method to make a living, then there are a few things that are required to make this happen. These include:

- Some sort of access to a trading desk.
  This tool is often reserved for those traders who work for a larger company or those who will manage a lot of money. The dealing desk provides these traders with the ability to do trades instantaneously which is very important to the success of day trading. If you don't work for a large financial organization, you may need to discuss with your broker what options are available for you here.

- Several news sources.
  The news is going to provide you with the information you need to pick the best trades in

day trading. You need to be one of the first to know when something big is about to happen. Then, you can jump in the market in the beginning and get a good price. Once everyone else catches onto the news, you can sell your security and make a profit. Having at least three or four news sources that you look through each day can help you figure out the right trades to make.

- Analytical software.

  When it comes to day trading, analytical software is going to be so critical. It may be a bit expensive when you get started but it is a necessity for most day traders. For those who are working on swing trades or technical indicators, you will rely more on this software than the news. Some of the features that you will want to find in your software include:

  - Pattern recognition that is automatic.

    This means that when you work with the trading program, you want it to identify technical indicators such as channels and flags. You may even want some complex indicators such as the Elliot Wave patterns.

o Neural and genetic applications.
These are programs that will utilize genetic and neural networks to help make your trading systems better. They are good at making more accurate predictions when you are trying to figure out where the price is going to move in the future.

o Broker integration.
Some software applications are going to make it possible to interface directly with the brokerage. This makes it easier for an individual trader to do an automatic execution of trades. Not only does this help you to get into and out of the markets at the right time, but it can also take some of the emotions out of the game.

o Backtesting.

Backtesting can be useful because it allows a trader to practice a bit. You will take your strategy and test out how it would have worked if you used it in the past. This is not always completely accurate, especially if the market turns a different way. But in some cases, it can give you an idea of how your current strategy will work in the market by basing the information on historical data.

When these tools are combined, they can provide a trader with a big edge over others in the marketplace. And when it comes to working with day trading, they are really important. Without them, many traders without the right experience can lose money in the market.

How Is Day Trading Different Than Swing Trading and from Long-Term Investing

If you have ever researched other forms of investing or have done any other forms, then you will find that day trading can be a little bit different than the others. There are a lot of different types of investing that you can do and understanding how they are all different can make a difference in how you approach this kind of trading.

First, there is day trading. Day trading is when you get into the market at some point during the day. It can be any time that you want but most people choose to enter after the first five minutes are done to avoid any issues with the volatility in the market. Then, at some point during the day, you will exit the market. This can happen a few minutes after you do the initial trade, it could take a few hours, or you will wait until the end of the day. How long you stay in the market will depend on how well it is doing and the strategy that you picked.

Day traders will look at short-term charts to figure out moving averages, resistance and support lines, and to make better decisions in investing. Outside of news that happens right within a company, they will not concern themselves with how the company will work in the future or what changes will happen beyond that day.

The biggest thing here is that you enter the market and exit the market all in the same day. You should never leave your position open overnight. Doing this results in different strategies and is actually swing trading. Swing trading is similar to day trading but it takes place over a longer period of time. Most swing traders will last between two days and two weeks. This gives you a little more time to prepare and make your moves but it is still pretty fast paced. You will hold the position overnight but if your profits don't happen within a few weeks, you need to exit.

Swing traders are going to focus their energy on preparing for a big trend. You are going to look at the news and other indicators to figure out the best times to enter the market because a big change is about to happen with a company within the next few weeks. These traders enter before others catch on to the change, getting the stock for a good price. Then, when everyone else is alerted to the news and rushes to purchase the stock, the swing trader can sell their stock and make a huge profit as well.

Then there is long-term investing. This is often what is done for those who want to earn an income from quarterly dividends in the company they invest in, or those who are looking to invest to help out with their retirement. They are looking for the long-term trend of a company and hoping that it goes up over many years rather than over a few hours and they don't really look at the daily ups and downs for a company.

With long-term investing, you are going to need to look more at the fundamentals of the company, rather than the technical parts. This helps you to determine whether the company is secure, if they will continue on the path they currently follow, or if there are any concerns that you need to focus on before investing in that company.

Day trading is very different from some of the other forms of investing but it is still very appealing to different investors. It provides an opportunity to really learn about the market and to make money quickly, as long as you are able to use the system in the proper manner.

The Benefits of Day Trading

There are traders who recommend against getting into day trading. They worry that day trading is too risky, too fast-paced, and that it is too hard to actually make any money with this form of trading. There are actually a lot of benefits that come from day trading as long as you know how to read the charts and how to do an accurate trade. Some of the benefits that you can get from day trading include the following:

- Day trading can eliminate some of your overnight risks.
  Depending on how the market does, there can be fluctuations that go between five and ten percent. The stock that is making a higher low and a higher high, and which even closed that

day at a new high, has the ability to open up the next day at a low level. In one night, if things don't go right, you could wipe out all of your profit. And this all happens when you are sleeping! This doesn't happen with day trading because all of the trades happen and finish in one day. Political developments, disasters, and news are not going to disturb you. You can finish the trade and then go to bed without worries.

- You can use leverage.
  Many brokers will offer you several times more than your capital margin. This provides you with more opportunities to control more investment than is available. If you are careful with your trading, this is a good way to multiply the profits that you can make. Leveraging is not usually recommended for beginners because it could result in you losing a ton of money as well but it is something to consider.

- Gives you a better chance to learn about the market.

Because you are doing a lot of trades each day, this is a great way to help you test out some trading patterns and learn more about the market.

- It can be done at home.
  You can technically do day trading from home around your own time. You would just enter and exit the trades around your other obligations. Or, if you get good enough at this type of trading, you would just work this when you want to and can get all the profits in your free time.

- The satisfaction of the different challenges.
  Many traders find that the continuous changes in the market can give them a feeling of accomplishment. It is an adrenaline surge that they enjoy and that keeps them working on this kind of market.

The Negatives of Day Trading

While many traders are able to make a good income with day trading, it is not the best for every trader. Some traders may want to work more with a long-term option. They may be interested in something that has a little less risk. Or maybe they aren't interested in being hooked to the computer and worrying about all the little shifts that occur in the market and how it affects their current trade. Some of the disadvantages that show up for some traders who are considering day trading include:

- During market hours, this trading takes a lot of intense focus.
  If you have a lot of trouble focusing for a long period of time, or there are obligations that make it hard for you to do this, day trading can be frustrating. Day trading includes a lot of staying on your toes to figure out when the best setups are going to come along.

- You may miss out on some overnight gaps.

As many professional traders will tell you, there is a lot of money being left on the table when it comes to those overnight gaps.

- The market may move a lot but that doesn't mean your trade will move.
  This happens often when we talk about day trading. This depends on how often the market makes a big move and then you either have a loss or barely break even. As a new trader, this may not make much sense, but it does matter with day trader.

- The market hours aren't the best for everyone.
  Those who live on the east coast may have no problem with the hours but if you live in any of the other time zones, it can sometimes be difficult and inconvenient to trade in the U.S. markets. Some like this time difference though because they can get up early in the morning and get some good deals. Either way, you will have to watch the market and make the times work for wherever you are.

- There are a lot of opportunities for the trader to over trade.

  Overtrading, either taking too many opportunities than you can handle or trading too big, is often something that happens with day trading. If you lack some self-discipline, remember there are always other trading methods to go with. The extra buying power that comes with this method of trading can give you a loose leash. If you have a lot of issues with staying disciplined, the temptation to overtrade could lead to your demise and a lot of lost money.

- You may spend too much on trading costs and commissions.

  This can end up costing you a lot of money if you are not careful. Any time that you shorten up the timeframe you are working with which can come up with day trading, those commissions can sometimes cause issues.

- You will need more software than other forms of trading.

A good day trader will have some charting software, a scanner, and a broker to help them evaluate all the different choices that they can pick from. You can do day trading without this but it becomes a lot harder when you do.

Day trading can be a great way for you to make money but there are some situations where it is not the best option for you. Explore how day trading works and some of the positives and negatives before determining if it is the right trading method for you.

The Basics of Day Trading in Futures

Many people think of day trading as working with stocks. While this is one option you can choose, some people like to work with other options, such as futures. Futures can be effective because there isn't going to be a restriction on shorting when you work in this market.

First, let's look at what futures are. Futures are going to be financial contracts that will obligate a buyer to purchase their asset or a seller to sell their asset. This can be a physical commodity or a financial instrument. They differ from options, that is, you have to buy and sell these if you enter the contract, while an option will let you choose if you want to buy or sell. The contracts for these futures will detail the quality and the quality of the asset you are purchasing, and you simply need to set up the time limit of these to be for one day, rather than over a few weeks or months, or even years, to make it day trading.

While a day trading strategy for futures will often have many components and can be analyzed for how profitable it is in may ways, it is often going to be ranked based on the win rate, or the reward to risk ratio. The win rate is how many trades won based off all the trades that you did. So if you win 55 out of 100 trades, your win rate is 55 percent. As a day trader, having a win rate above 50 percent is pretty good. You can also work with the reward to risk ratio. This helps you determine how much risk you have to take to get a certain profit.

Since you are required to purchase or sell the future based on the contract you pick, it is important to pick a day that has a lot of volatility. This ensures that the price has time to go the direction that you want before you have to sell off. If the market isn't moving much, you may have to sell before you can make a good profit, or purchase when the price is too high.

Day trading with the Forex market

Another market that you can consider using when it comes to a day trading strategy is to trade in the Forex market. The forex market is a global decentralized market that allows traders to invest in currencies. This includes all the aspects of buying, selling, or even exchanging currencies at a determined price. In terms of the volume of trading, it is the largest market in the world. The main participants in this market will be international banks. But some individual investors choose to get into the market and make money as well.

Trading in the forex market is a great way to take advantage of changes in one economy over another. You will find that it is very similar to trading stocks and other options, but with day trading, you will really need to pay attention to the market and watch when the price of one currency goes up or down. Some of the basic guidelines that you can follow when you choose to day trade with forex will include:

- Trade just when the US and London markets are open. You may only want to trade for a few hours a day, usually when the two markets open. This helps you to not get worn out and make mistakes.
- When you trade, work with the one minute charts. This helps you to keep up wit the small changes.
- Only trade in the same direction of the trend. You won't be in the market long enough to worry about anything else.
- Wait for a pullback. This pullback needs to stall out at some point or show some signs that the price is starting to move back in the trending

direction. This must happen before it reaches a major prior swing low.

- When you see a pullback, your price needs to consolidate, which means that it must move sideways for at least two bars. Then you can purchase a breakout that is above the high price of this consolidation. This can take some patience because it may not stall the whole way and you may have to wait for some time.

- Put in those targets and stop losses. These ensure that you are going to get the best results and won't lose too much money.

- If you hear that there is a major news event that is about to happen, you need to leave all of your positions a minimum of two minutes ahead of that. You don't want to trade again until after the news is released, so even cancel all pending orders when you hear of new news or when you plan to be away from the computer. This makes sure that you aren't going to stay in the market and get on the wrong side of consumer sentiment about the news.

- Create a good day trading routine. This keeps you on track and can help you avoid some mistakes in the process.

There are some investors who want to trade in other markets, but usually until you become more accustomed to working in day trading, it is best to stay with the US market. this way, it is easier for you to get the news that you need to make informed decisions.

Day trading with cryptocurrencies

A newer option you can choose for day trading is cryptocurrencies. These cryptocurrencies are taking over the world and many people are starting to notice. There are thousands of these currencies available and they offer security, anonymity, and a great way to make a profit if you use them the right way. And since their volatility is high, you can easily make a lot of profit in a short amount of time.

You have to be careful with this kind of investing though. There are no regulations on the currency and they aren't available on the stock market. They also have a lot of ups and downs with them so it is also easy to lose your money quickly if you aren't careful. You really need to do your due diligence here because with so many options of cryptocurrencies to work with, many of them are not strong, and many can be fakes. And since these currencies aren't regulated, you won't be able to get anyone to help you out if you pick the wrong type of currency.

Now, if you take the right precautions and are willing to watch the market to protect your money, cryptocurrencies can be perfect for earning money with day trading. In fact, after seeing the crash of Bitcoin in January 2018 after the currency reached almost $20,000 and then crashed to under $10,000 in a few days, investing in these currencies over the long-term isn't the best. But the high volatility in these currencies make them perfect to join into the cryptocurrency market, stay in for a few hours, and then get out and make a good profit in the process.

If you do decide to invest in cryptocurrencies, make sure that you take some time to research charts and the history of that currency. There won't be any reports from the SEC for you to read through and make informed decisions. Instead, you need to look online, read the charts, and learn the patterns of the currency on your own. But a smart investor who is willing to take the time and learn can make a big profit in no time.

Some cryptocurrencies, such as Bitcoin, are more established and can be great options to go with. Others are newer and you may need to do your research on as well. You also need to check the amount of variation that comes with the market. if you are only going to make a few dollars on a trade, it may not be worth your time. Just like with your broker, these cryptocurrency markets are going to charge you to exchange your fiat money with the cryptocurrency of your choice.

Chapter 2:
The Basics of Performing a Trade

Before you jump into the world of day trading, it is important to know some of the basics that come with investing. You don't want to start out on your first trade and then find that you don't even know what the different terms mean, or you can't read the charts that are needed to make profitable trades. For example, it is important for you to know what a "bid and ask' is as well as what the different order types that traders can place when they are ready to buy and sell in the market. Here we are going to explore some of these terms, and what they mean, so you can take your trade by storm when you are ready.

Bid and Ask

If you headed over to a financial website and type in the ticker symbol for a stock, there would be a lot of numbers that show up. You would see words like market cap, EPS, div and yield, beta, volume, 52 wk range, previous close, and more. This information is referred to as the level one information and it provides you with facts about the best available price for a stock at a certain time. Let's look at an example of this by looking at Intel (INTC) Corporation's stock information. If we did, some of the information that we would see includes:

- EPS – 2.30

  This will show how profitable the company is.

- Market cap – 273.41B

  This is what the company is valued at currently in the market.

- Div and Yield – 1.20/2.10%

  This is the percentage of dividends that the company will pay out each year.

- Volume – 31,183,166.00

  This is how many shares have been bought and sold for this company.

- Beta – 1.207

  This is going to indicate how volatile the market is for that stock. When it is above one, it means that the stock is more volatile than the market.

- P/E – 24.82

  This is going to be the price to earnings ratio that is found when you divide the market value and the EPS.

- 52 Wk Range: 33.23-57.10

  This is going to show the lowest and the highest price that this stock has reached over the past year.

- Days Range: 55.80-57.10

  This is going to be the lowest and highest price that the stock has reached through the last trading day.

- Open – 55.84

  This is the price that the stock opened at last.

- Prev Close – 55.20

This is the price that the stock closed at.

When you are picking out the stock you want to trade with, you will want to take a close look at these numbers. These can show you how much the stock is moving (or how volatile so you know you can sell it later), and you can learn if the stock is likely to go above its current value. All of this information will come together to help you pick the perfect stocks to make a good profit from in day trading.

Types of Orders

When you enter into day trading, there are going to be several types of orders that you can pick. Some of the most common are shown below.

Market Order

This is an order to sell or purchase a stock at the best bid or to ask when an order gets to the market. A lot of traders like this type of order because it is seen as the fastest option. However, this isn't always the truth. It will guarantee that you get an execution but it can make it so that you get into or out of the trade faster than everybody else.

You should work to avoid this as much as you can. You really want to have more control over the trade than what the market order can provide. If you have someone else who is watching the trade for you, or you absolutely can't watch your own trades, it may work. But it is better to go with a different option when day trading.

Limit Order

With a limit order, you are setting it up to buy or sell when the stock reaches a certain price, or if it is sold or can be purchased at a better price than what you set. This is the order that most traders will go with. It ensures that they get the stock for the best price and that they can sell it for an even better price.

Some traders won't work with this option because they are worried that if they use it, the order won't get executed. They think the program will just miss out on their requests waiting for a good price. With this order though, the program will be set up to place your trade at any level that you want.

Stop Order

The stop order is an order that will become a market order as soon as a certain price is hit. This is often a method that a trader will use in order to limit losses and can really protect the profits of the trader. You still need to watch what the market is doing and make sure that you know what is going on with your trade the whole time. Since the market can change in just seconds though, the stop order can be a great way to stop the trade before you lose too much money and can't do anything to prevent it.

As a new trader, it is important to know how each of these orders works. Start by studying the information in the first section and learning how you can use it to make a good trade. From there, you can place the right order for the trade that you are going to work on. Just remember that these trades are very short-term, ranging from a few seconds to no longer than one day. But when you know how the market works and pick the right stocks with the right orders, you can easily get some great results and some great profits.

Chapter 3:
Opening up a Brokerage Account

In order to execute the trades that you want, you will need to open up a brokerage account. There are varieties of factors that are going to come into play when you pick out a brokerage account including the margin rates, the commissions you will owe, and any other fees the company tacks on. If you pick a bad broker or one who takes too many fees from you, it doesn't matter how successful you are with your trades; they will end up taking most, if not all, of the profits that you make.

If you plan to be a high-volume trader, you could end up paying a ton of commission fees each day to the broker. For those who plan to trade in high volume which is more common with day trading compared to other forms of trading, you will need to contact your broker and see what the rates are. Make sure to ask about all their fees and if they have any incentives or specials that could end up saving you money.

After you have a good idea about the costs and fees you will have with a broker, you will need to take a look at the platforms they have to offer. These platforms are very important because they could affect things like price quotes and execution speed for your trades. As a day trader, even a few seconds of delay in the processing can cost you a lot of money. Many brokers will have executions that happen in real time but there are times when slippage can happen. You should test out the brokerage's platform to see if it is comfortable and if you like how it works.

Take some time to look at the financial stability and customer service of the brokers you are considering. You want to pick out a brokerage that has great customer service because if a crisis happens, you want help quickly. Financial strength can be important because there are brokers who have gone out of business, and if yours does, it may cost you the entire amount that is in your account.

There are many different brokers you can consider using for your trading needs. Some of the best ones that you may want to work with include:

- MB Trading
- SpeedTrader
- Generic Trade
- OptionsXpress
- E-Trade
- Fidelity
- TD Ameritrade
- Lightspeed
- TradeStation
- Interactive Brokers

After you choose the broker you want to work with, you can set up your account, and add money. Most brokerages will require you to have money in your account before you even start with any trades. Take some time here to explore all the features that come with your new trading account, checking out the different graphs, the interactive tools and more. Then, when you are ready (and after you have taken a look through the rest of this book), you can start using your strategy to make money with day trading.

When you are setting up your brokerage account, you need to make sure that you watch out for some of the fees that you incur. Each brokerage account, even if you do most of the work by yourself, is going to charge some fees for doing the trades. You need to know what all of these are before you even think about trading, or you could lose all your profits just to pay for the brokerage account.

Some brokerage accounts will charge a base fee for each trade that you do. This can often get expensive especially since day trading relies on you being able to do a ton of little trades throughout the day. This is often not the best option in fees to go with unless you are a long-term trader who doesn't plan to get out of the market for some time. Most day traders will go on a commission basis so they only have to pay when they make a profit. When doing your strategies, make sure to factor in the fees or the commissions that you have to pay, and take those out of your profits when determining how profitable a trade is.

Chapter 4:
Finding the Right Stocks to Trade

While we are going to explore some of the best strategies to use when you work in day trading, first, we need to have an idea of how to pick out the right stock to make day trading easier. You can have the best strategy in the world but if you pick the wrong stock, then you are wasting your time. Before you go any further, you will need to take some time here to study your stocks. The following factors below will help you pick out the perfect stocks to trade.

The Revenue of the Company

The growth of a stock is going to begin when the company starts to make money. If the company isn't making any money, then they may be brand new and it's too early to figure out how profitable they will be or they are about to fail. Either way, you won't really make money in day trading with them. The revenue is going to provide you with an idea of how much money a company is making. If you look at the revenue and see that it is consistently going up, this is a good sign that the company is growing.

- Fail.
  If you see that the revenue of the company is decreasing, then the stock fails and you shouldn't use it for trading.

- Pass.
  If you see that the revenue is going up, then the stock passes and may be right for trading.

Earnings per Share

The Earnings per share, or EPS, is going to show how much of the company's revenue is flowing out and into the pocket of its stockholders. The EPS is going to be the amount of money the company makes in profits per share of stock that it has.

- Fail.

If you see the EPS score is going down, then the stock fails.

- Pass.
  If you see that the EPS score is going up, then the stock passes.

The Return on Equity

The return on equity is very important when it comes to picking out the stock that you will invest your money in. The ROE can be a good indicator of how efficiently the management of a company is able to produce returns.

- Fail.
  If you see that the ROE is going down, especially if it has gone down over the past two years, then the stock fails.

- Pass.

If you notice that the ROE has been going up for at least the past two years in a row, then the stock passes.

Analyst Recommendations

You should take some time to hear what the analysts in the market say about a certain stock. While there are times when these analysts will miss out on important information or may miss out on a great opportunity, they do spend a lot of time researching the stock market. And when they are done, they will provide their recommendations. This can be useful information for a beginner in day trading:

- Fail.
  The recommendation fails if the consensus recommendation doesn't reach the buy level.

- Pass.
  The recommendation is going to pass if the consensus recommendation is to purchase.

Positive Earnings Surprise

Each quarter the company needs to release a statement about their finances. This is a legal requirement for them to be on the stock exchange and it provides investors and lenders will some important information about the finances of the company. Before a company releases these statements, many analysts will make some predictions about the ESP for the company:

- Fail.
  If the earnings during the previous quarters for the company have been negative, then the stock fails.

- Pass.
  If the earnings do come in and they are higher than what was predicted, then they pass.

Earnings Forecast

As a day trader, it is important to have a good idea of what the company could potentially earn in the future.

This will help you determine if anyone is likely to want to purchase the stocks later on.

- Fail.
  The stock will fail if the forecasted EPS is going to decrease.

- Pass.
  The stock will pass if the forecasted EPS increases.

Earnings Growth

This is the number that a trader can use because it tells you how the analysts believe the earnings of a company will grow each year.

- Fail.
  If the long-term five-year number is under eight percent, then the stock fails.

- Pass.

If the forecast for the long-term five-year number ends up being over eight percent, then the stock passes.

PEG Ratio

Another number that you can look at is the PEG ratio. This is a ratio that will include the P/E along with other factors that were important in the growth for a company. As a trader, you want to make sure that you are working with stocks that are predicted to grow in the future, so this ratio can be really important in determining this information:

- Fail.

  If the ratio value is more than 1.0, then the stock fails your analysis.

- Pass.

  If the ratio value is less than 1.0, then the stock passes.

Industry Price Earnings

The industry price earnings will show you the average of how much the company earns as compared to other companies in the same industry. This can help you to find out if the company is doing as good as, worse than, or better than other companies at that time:

- Fail.
  The stock fails if the P/E ends up lower than the industry's earnings for that time period.

- Pass.
  The stock passes if their P/E ends up higher than the industry's earnings.

Days to Cover

The short interest is going to help you know the number of shares that investors are short on. The days of cover will refer to how many days it will take the short sellers to cover the position that they are in. This information can help you get a good idea on whether the company is profitable, how long it would take them to become profitable, and if this is really a good investment opportunity for you to work with.

- Fail.
  If the days to cover ends up higher than two, then it is going to fail your analysis.

- Pass.
  If the days to cover ends up lower than two, then it is going to pass your analysis.

The more items that a particular stock is able to pass, the better option it is for day trading and making you a profit. With that being said, there are times when it is very hard for you to find a stock that is going to work with all of these different aspects, and you may have to decide which ones are the most important for your trading strategies. Try to hit as many, if not all, of these as possible to get the best stock for your trading needs.

Each trader is going to have their own strategy when it comes to picking out the right stocks to go with. We will talk about a few strategies to use in a few chapters, and sometimes these strategies will lead you to the right stock for your needs. But looking at the ten factors above can really make a difference in answering the question "What stock should I invest in?"

Chapter 5:
Picking the Best Time to Trade

As a day trader, whether you are a beginner trader or a professional, you need to start relying on consistency. This is going to make it easier for you to pick the right stocks to invest in and can help you figure out if you are going to make a profit or not. For example, a stock that has consistent ups and downs in the market will be much easier to invest in because you know when the high and the low points will occur. A stock that is really volatile and doesn't have a pattern at all can be hard to invest in because you never know where it will go from one day to the next. There are a few tips that you can follow to make picking the best time to trade an easier decision.

When you want to trade in stocks, the best time to do this is the first two hours after your chosen market has opened, and then in the last hours before closing. So, trading between 9:30 and 11:30 is a good time to begin.

This time is very volatile, which can give you a lot of price changes and a lot of potentials to make profits. Then, you can also consider trading at three to four in the afternoon because some big movements can occur at these times as well. For traders who can't spend all day trading and who only have a few hours available, the morning session is the best option.

If you are looking to trade in futures, when the market opens is the best time to trade. Active futures have trading activity all of the time, so the best opportunities for this will often start earlier than when the stock market opens. Try to focus your energy on trading between 8:30 to 11:00. The official time for closing the futures market can vary but you can also look at trading during the last hour as well.

During the week, the forex market is available for trading all day long. The most popular day trading pair that you may want to work with is EUR/USD. The time when the forex market is the most volatile is between six and five GMT. For a day trader who wants to work with the forex market, you should focus most of your energy on trading during that time. Often, the biggest changes in prices will occur from 12 PM to 3 PM GMT. This is when both the US and the London markets are open which means that both groups are doing a lot of trading at the same time.

Despite the common belief about day trading, you don't have to spend all day on the computer doing your trades, unless you want to. This can be hard to keep up with and may end up leading you to a lot of anxiety and stress. Chances are, many traders are going to be more consistent and make more profits if you only spend a few hours trading in the market each day. Going with some of the times that we have listed above, depending on the market you want to trade in, can make a big difference.

Overall, you can earn a profit when you trade any time of the day as long as you have a good trading strategy and you know when to enter and when to exit the market. So if there is some reason why you can't be available right at the beginning or right at the end of the market, then don't fret about it too much. You can always trade at the time that works best for you.

Chapter 6:
How to Reduce Your Risks When Day Trading

Like any kind of investment, day trading does come with some risks. And day trading is often considered an even riskier option compared to some of the other investments you can choose. As a beginner, these risks may seem overwhelming and you may worry that this is not the right investment vehicle for you. There are a few things that you can do to help limit your risks as much as possible, including the following.

Only Trade What You Can Afford to Lose

When you enter a trade, make sure that you only trade the amount of money that you are comfortable with losing. There is a chance, especially when you are a beginner, when you may pick a bad trade and can lose money in the process. If you bet too much money on this, if you used leverage, or you made false assumptions about how the market would go, you could end up in big financial straights in the end.

Before you enter into day trading, consider setting aside a savings account. Take some time to put some money in savings before you get started, and add to it as you make profits. Only use the money in this account when you are trading. That way, when it is gone, you stop. And you didn't put your regular income or regular savings in jeopardy in the process.

Set up Your Stop Loss Points

Before you go into a trade, it is important to set up your entry and exit points. These are going to help maximize your profits like minimizing the potential losses that you could have. You need to have an idea of what price point the stock needs to be at for you to enter the trade. And then you need to have stop points for both ends of the spectrum for your profits and your losses.

Setting a stop point for losses can ensure that you only lose so much money. There are times when the market will plummet very quickly. If you don't have this in place, the market could slip down and you could lose a ton of money in a short amount of time. This stop point tells the brokerage account when you want to leave the market so you can limit your losses as much as possible.

You also want an exit strategy when it comes to how much money you want to make as profits. While this may seem silly as a trader, you want to earn as much as possible. But since there is a lot of variability in the market during the day, the market can often reach a high point and turn, without going back up again. Setting this point helps you to earn as much profit as possible without you staying in the market too long.

Work with a Broker

As a beginner, it is often best to work with a broker if you can. This can open up a lot of different resources to you that can make day trading more profitable. The right broker can be someone you bounce ideas off, someone you can ask questions to, and someone who can give you advice on the best stocks to follow for your trading.

You can also pick your broker based on the fees that they charge. Each broker is going to be a little different. Some charge a flat rate based on how many trades that you want to do. If you plan to do a lot of trades here, which is common for day trading, you may not want to go with that option. If you are spending $4 for every trade you do, this is going to add up quickly when you do a bunch of trades through that broker.

Another option is to work on commission with the broker. This way, you only pay a percentage of the profits that you earn on the trades you do. This can be helpful as long as you make sure that you earn enough on the trades that you can cover the commissions and fees, and still have some money left over for profits in your pockets.

Stick with the Strategy You Chose Through the Whole Trade

After you take a look through some of the strategies we will discuss in this guidebook, you should have an idea of which one will work the best for you. Make sure to pick one that makes sense for you, has the number of risks that you are willing to take, and that works with your trading profile.

Once you pick a trading strategy, you need to stick with it, at least during that trade. Many beginner traders end up failing and losing a lot of money because they enter a trade using one strategy and then they move into a second strategy at some point during the same trade. Sometimes this is because they see they will lose money and they want to make changes to prevent this. Other times, they do it simply because they didn't fully understand the strategy they chose. Either way, it can result in disaster for that trade.

If you start with a trading strategy and find that it is not the right one for you, then finish of the trade and try a new strategy on the next trade. You may lose some money on that first trade, but you will limit the loss quite a bit compared to switching strategies right in the middle.

Take a Break from Trading When You Need It

Sometimes, you are going to run into a trade that is bad. You may not have put in the right exit points, or you may have picked the wrong strategy and it didn't work out well for you. This can be hard especially if you are a new trader and it is one of your first trades.

After this bad trade happens, or if you seem to be making bad trade after bad trade, it is time to take a break. At this point, if you stay in the market, you will let your emotions take over and you will continue to make bad trading decisions. You may want to make a lot of income from day trading but sticking in the market when your emotions are involved, and after having a bad time with trading, it's just going to make things worse.

The break doesn't have to be a long time. Even a few days to a week can be enough to help you refocus and come back with a fresh look on your trading. It can be hard to take a break. You want to try a new idea, you want to make the money you lost back, and you don't want to give up. But taking a break doesn't mean you have given up. It simply means that you are giving yourself time to think critically the next time you trade.

Learn How to Keep the Emotions out of the Game

With any type of trading, if you let your emotions get into the game, then you have lost. This can be hard for many people especially if they put more money than they can afford to lose into a trade. With day trading, emotions can be an even bigger issue because the market changes so rapidly and you have to get in and out as quickly as possible.

When you allow your emotions to start coming into play, you are basically losing all of your control to make smart decisions. No one can make good decisions when the emotions are involved, and with all the stress and issues that can come with day trading, those emotions will hit some extremes pretty quickly. This is why it is so important to go through and pick out a winning strategy and to stick with it. This will keep the emotions at bay and you can make the decisions ahead of time before the emotions of being in the market come into play.

If you are in a trade and find that your emotions are starting to get in your way, it is time to make some changes. In some cases, you will be able to stick with your stop points and be safe for the rest of the trade. But if you have already gone through and left the stop points behind, it is time to leave the trade, no matter where it is going, and restart. You may even need to take a little time off from day trading, especially after a trade that did not do that well, so that you can regroup and get back to the critical thinking.

Don't Follow the Trends

If you are jumping onto a stock that everyone else is as well, then you are already getting to the party too late.

As soon as others start purchasing or selling a stock, the price has already changed and you are too late. This could result in you paying too much for a stock, or selling it for too little because you got caught up in the trend.

As a day trader, it is your job to learn to spot trends before they happen. If you read the news, look through the right charts, and use your knowledge about the market, you can easily jump onto a stock before the trend happens. When you do this successfully, you would then purchase the stock while the price is lower, before others catch on. Then, when others catch onto the value of that stock, the price will go up where you can sell it for a higher price than you originally purchased it.

You can use this idea when selling the stock as well. If you know that a stock has a price ceiling of $55 and the stock is currently at $54.99, or even above $55, then it is time to sell. In the short trading period that you get with day trading, you won't really see the price of a stock go much above its ceiling price ever. You can see this trend and sell the stock at that high point before the market drags it back down and you lose money.

Day traders do not jump onto a trend because they know it means that they are too late for the party on that particular security. They learn how to read the trends through their own research and can accurately predict the best times to purchase and sell the stock to make the most profit.

Chapter 7: Day Trading Strategy 1 – The Candlestick Strategy

Now that we have spent some time talking about day trading and how to get started, it is time to start talking about some of the strategies that you can use to become successful in day trading. Day trading is difficult and if you do not take the time to pick a good strategy and learn it fully, it will become harder. The first strategy that we will take a look at is the candlestick strategy. There are a few options that come with it and it often depends on which direction you think the market will go.

To create a candlestick chart, you need a few things. These things include:

- The opening price.
- The highest price in your chosen time frame.
- The lowest price that happens in that same time frame.

- The closing price values for each time period that you want to show.

While you can work with the candlestick strategy with pretty much any kind of trading that you want, for the purposes of this guidebook, you need to make sure that you pick some time frame that fits into your day. Some people will pick a time period that lasts the full day, some choose to go for a few hours, or you can go down to just a few minutes. Just make sure that the time frame you pick is consistent.

The hollow, or the filled out part of your chart, is going to be known as the body, while the thin lines that you can see above or below the body will show you the low and high ranges. These lines are known as the shadows, tails, or wicks of your candlesticks.

The high part of this chart is going to be marked by the top of your upper shadow while the low by the bottom of the lower shadow. If you see that a chosen stock is closing higher than it opened at, then you can go into the chart and draw a hollow candlestick at the bottom of the body. This bottom is going to represent what the opening price was and then the top will show the closing price.

There are also times when the stock will close at a price that is lower than what it opened at. This is when you will fill the candlestick at the top of the body being the opening price and then the bottom will be your closing price.

One thing that beginner traders need to remember is that the hollow candlesticks that have a close that is higher than the open means that there is a little bit of buying pressure in the market. If there is a filled candlestick where the close comes out as less than the open, it means that there is a little bit of selling pressure.

Bullish Candlesticks

Now that we know a little bit more about these candlesticks, it is time to look into a few of the different ones that you can work with. One of the nice things about this strategy is that you can use it in any type of economy, regardless of if the economy goes up or down. You just need to find the right candlestick strategy to make that happen.

The first type of candlestick that you can look at is the bullish candlestick. Any candle that has a larger body near the top will be seen as bullish. This means that the buyers are in control of the price of that stock. When you notice that, this chart is going on realize that the buyers are the ones who keep pushing on the market to make the price go up higher and higher. This candlestick is not going to really tell you the price that the security will go up to but it will tell you that the bulls are winning and that they have the power, for now, to determine where the price will go.

Bearish Candlesticks

On the other side of things, there are also bearish candles. These are a bit different compared to the bullish candlesticks and you will want to trade in a different manner. When we look at a bearish candle, it means that instead of the buyers being in charge, the sellers will be able to control the price action for the market. Purchasing the stock at this time is not a great idea but if you already own the security, now is the time to sell.

When you look at the charts and see that there is a candle that is filled in and the body is pretty long, this means that the opening for that security was high, but the closing dropped down. This is the best way to tell that the market is currently bearish and it is not a great time for traders to get into it, unless they want to spend way too much on the security and not earn much, if any, profit.

Indecision Candlesticks

Another type of candlestick that you may run across is known as the indecision candlestick. There are two main types of these candlesticks known as Dojis and spinning tops. To understand what these indecision candlesticks are about, let's take a look at each type.

The Spinning Top

The first indecision candle that you can work with is called spinning tops. These are candles that have high wicks that look similar in size along with some low wicks that are larger on the bottom and show up as indecisive. With the spinning top, the sellers and the buyers have powers that are close to even, which means the stock could go either way. No one, neither the sellers nor the buyers, is in control over how the price will go at this time, but there is a fight to figure out who is going to win. The volume on these is often lower because the traders want to wait. No one wants to get in here and find out that they guessed wrong and that the wrong party takes over control of the price.

The trend in the price is going to show up shortly after you see the spinning top, so the decision is made fast. Once the fight is won, whether it is by the buyers or sellers, the price is going to start its new trend. This is why it is important as a trader to look at and recognize this kind of price action. Of course, it is better to wait a bit before trading in the market and then see which way things will go. If the price starts to move up, you can jump on because the price is going up. But if the price goes down, you should wait a bit and see if the market goes back up before you make a purchase.

Dojis

Another type of indecision candlestick you can work with is known as a Doji. There are a few shapes and forms of this candlestick, but they end up having nobody to your candlestick in the graph, or the body is pretty small to start with. When you look at your charts and see that there is a Doji present there, it means that there is a big fight going on between your buyers and sellers and no one is coming out the winner in it yet.

There are some exceptions to this though. There are times when the Doji does show a bottom and a top wick, but these are not going to be equal. If the top wick is longer, this means that the buyer is trying to push the price higher but they were met with failure on this. This is sometimes an indicator that the buyers are not holding onto the power and the sellers may try to control the price.

You may also see some charts were the wick on the bottom is the longer one. With this, it means that the seller was trying to control the price but they were met with failure on this. This means that it is more likely there will be a takeover price by the buyers.

You can definitely use this to help you see what trends are going on. If one of these candlesticks shows up during a bullish trend, it means that the bulls are wearing out and now the bears are trying to take over control of the price. If this candlestick forms when there is a bearish downward trend, it suggests that now the bears are tired and now the buyers or the bulls will take over the price. This can help you to see when a trend is about to occur in the market and can help you to make some smart decisions.

The candlestick pattern is a great way to predict how the market is going. When the market is going up based on these candlesticks, you will want to purchase and then sell before they go down. When the market is going down based on these candlesticks, you will either want to stay out of the market if you are not already in, or you will want to sell before the price goes down and you lose too much money. Take some time to learn how to make these charts and you will find that they are a fantastic way for you to monitor the way that the market is going.

Chapter 8: Day Trading Strategy 2 – The ABCD Pattern

As a beginner trader, you may want to consider working with the ABCD pattern because it is basic and easy to trade with. Although it has been around for some time and it is simple, it is still effective, which is why so many traders are still using it. With this strategy, you will do whatever the other traders in the market are doing because you believe that the trend is your friend. Let's take a look at how this one can work.

The ABCD pattern will start out with an upward move that is strong. At this time, the buyers are aggressively buying a stock from point A and making constantly new highs of the day, which is point B. You will want to get into the trade at this point but do not chase the trade since point B is already an unusually high price. Plus, at this point, you are not able to say where the stop loss should be and it is never a good idea to trade without setting the stop point.

At point B, the traders who already bought the stock at an earlier time will start to slowly sell their stocks to make some profit, and this will get the price to come down. It is not a good idea to enter into a trade at this time because you will not be able to guess where the pullback will happen. However, if you see that the price isn't coming down from a specific level, such as point C, this means that the stock is working with some potential support. This means that you will be able to plan the trade and then set up the stops that you need so that you make the most profit.

This is a simple strategy that you can choose which makes it a great option for beginners. There are a few steps that you can take to make this strategy more successful. These steps include:

- When you look through the scanner to find a stock, that surges up from its original point A and this reaches a new high for the day or its point B, you need to pay some attention. You will need to look at that stock and see if the new price is able to become a support than what was found at the original point A. If it does have enough support, this will then become point C for your trade. Be careful looking at this because you don't want to make an assumption and trade too early.

- After you have made your point C, you can watch the stock carefully throughout its consolidation period. From the information you glean during this time, you can choose the preferred share size to work with. This is a good time to come up with a good stop and exit strategy.

- When you see that the price is holding onto that support at point C, you should enter the trade at a point that is on or close to point C. The goal here is that your chosen security is going to move up to a new support point, known as point D, if not even higher.

- To work with this strategy, you want to have the stop loss end up at point C. If there is any time of the day where the price goes lower than your set point C, then you need to sell your stock and accept any losses that occur. The closer you can purchase the stock to that point C, the better with this strategy so that you can make sure your losses aren't too high.

- If you see that this stock continues to go higher, you will want to sell about half the position when it gets to point D. You can then move your stop higher to your entry point to help you make a profit.

- As soon as you see that the target is hit, or you see that the price is losing steam, even if it doesn't reach the goal, then you should sell the remaining shares that you have. When the price gets to a new low, this shows that the buyers are exhausted and the trend will go backward.

This strategy is a simple one you can work with but you need to really know how to read the charts you have and you must have the patience to enter the market at the right time to make a good profit. You also must be careful and watch the stock the whole time you are in the trade. The trend can easily turn on you and then you could have runaway losses. But as a beginner who can spend some time on the market and on your trade, you will see that the ABCD strategy is a great one to work with.

Chapter 9:
Day Trading Strategy 3 – Reversal Trading

The bottom and top reversal options are two trading strategies that a lot of day traders will rely on. This is because the reversal strategies will have defined exit and entry points, which gives you some clear guidelines about when you should get into the market and when you should leave the market. You will be able to find the best reversal setups using a scanner and indecision candlesticks will help you to set up your entry points and more so that you get the best results with the reversal trading.

When you are working with a reversal strategy, you will notice that there are four important elements that need to be present. These four elements include:

1. There needs to be a minimum of five candlesticks present on a five-minute chart.

They can be moving downward or upward, but they need to be present.

2. The stock will have an extreme five-minute Relative Strength Index indicator. If the RSI is above 90 or above 10, it should catch your interest. This RSI will compare the magnitude of recent losses or gains over a specified period of time to measure how fast and how much the price movement was. The values will be on a range from 0 to 100. This can be used to help you recognize a stock that is oversold or overbought. If the RSI is over 90, it shows that the conditions of the stock are overbought and if the RSI is below 10, it means that the conditions are oversold.

3. The stock is being traded near, or at least close, to an important support or resistant level.

4. Once you notice that there is a trend and that it is nearing its end which is something that you can see with those indecision candles, you are near the reversal. This is something that you as

a trader need to pay attention to and be ready for because it is time to finish out the trade at this point.

Remember those indecision candlesticks that we talked about earlier? We are going to bring those back now. When you work with reversal trading, you need to use these candlesticks. These will indicate that the current trend for a security is about to change. The Doji candlestick is a good one here because it can really show the changing trends.

For example, if you are looking through your charts and you see that there is a candle with a top tail, you can safely assume that during that market period the price did go up but the market didn't have enough power to hold the price at this level resulting in the stock being sold off. This kind of candlestick is going to show where the buyer lost the push-up the battle and soon the seller is going to control the price, which pushes everything back down.

This same process is shown when you go the other way as well. When the candle has a lower wick that is long, you can guess that during this period, the price ended up going down. But while going down, the price wasn't able to stay at these levels, so it was brought up again. With this battle, the sellers last the pushdown. The buyers are going to work to push that price up again.

With this kind of trading strategy, you should take a look at your chart for the indecision candlesticks because they let the trader know that the current trade is not going to stick around and things are going to change soon. But you must read the chart accurately so you can make sure that a reverse is going to happen. If you make the wrong trade, you are going to lose money in the process.

When an indecision candle or a Doji forms, you know that the reversal is about to happen. You can also look at the RSI to see if the numbers come in above 90 or below 10. Any time that this happens, you need to look for an actual entry that is near a strong support for the intraday when you work with the bottom reversal. But if you work with the top reversal, you want to look for the resistance level.

Since these work a bit differently, let's look at the bottom reversal first. For the bottom reversal, when you have a line of candles that is long and right next to each other and they are each working to make new lows, the first candle that shows up after this line that has a new high that is near its support level is the one that will be the most important. For many traders, this is the time when they will enter the market. This is early enough in the trade that you are still going to get a great price for the security but the one candle that went up shows that the trend is about to change and it won't take long before you can sell your security for a great profit.

With these bottom trades, you also need to look for the right exit indicators. These are simple. If you see that the stock goes up before going right back down, then it is time to step out and take a loss. The stock could stay down for some time and you don't want to end up with a bigger loss. If you purchase the stock based off this strategy and then the price goes sideways, realize that this usually results in the price of that stock going back down, and sometimes dropping lower again, so it is time to get out of the market. Even if this flatline only lasts for a few minutes, get out and save your money.

With this strategy, if you enter at the right time and things hold constant, you are going to make a profit. This trend can sometimes be short-term and other times it will keep going up. Have a few indicators in place so you know when to take your money and leave so you have a profit, but don't stay in so long that you start losing money.

For the reversal strategy above, the biggest thing that a trader can do is watch out for stocks that are moving up or down, and then also look to see if there are any support and resistance levels that can make for the perfect trading opportunity. This helps because it takes some of the impulses out of the mix and can reduce the times that you would just rush into the trade because you are excited.

To make this strategy easier to understand and follow, here are some of the steps that you can take with the reversal strategy:

- Turn on your scanner so that it looks for a chart that has at least four candlesticks with a downward trend. You can then look closer at this stock and check out the daily support and resistance levels to see if it is a good option.
- Don't just jump in at this point. You want to wait for some confirmation. First, you need to have the formation of a Doji or some other indecision candle. Then make sure that this chosen stock is traded near its intraday support level. Then look at the RSI and see if it is lower than 10.
- Continue to watch the stock at this point. When it comes to a new high at either minute 1 or minute 5, then you should purchase it.
- The profit target for this trade is either going to be the next support level, when the stock reaches a new low in the five minute periods, or the Volume Weighted Average price.

Another option to work with on this strategy is the top reversal. This is similar to what you find with the bottom reversal option but now we are working more with the short selling side. Here we are going to just look at the steps that come with this strategy to make it easier and help you see how the two reversal strategies are different.

- Set up the scanner as we did before but make sure that the four consecutive candlesticks are trending up. When this information hits the scanner, look at the volume and the daily level of your support and resistance to see if this is the right stock.
- The top reversal strategy also needs some confirmation. This could show up with an RSI that is above 90, or an indecision candle that is bearish.
- Once you look at the five-minute section and see that the stock has gone down to a new low, this shows that the market is having a weakness. This is the time for you to short sell your stocks.
- The stop for this one is going to be the high of your previous candlestick. Another option is to go with the high of the day.
- If you are looking for a profit target, you either need to take it out when the stock reaches a new support level, or when it reaches a new five minute high.

The reversal trade is a great one to go with and some traders will pick this as their only trading strategy because it is so successful. These strategies can actually take out some of the risks, as long as you use them properly, and you still have a good chance to make some higher profits. And since it works in both a bullish and a bearish market, you can use this reversal strategy no matter what the market is doing on a particular day.

Chapter 10:
Day Trading Strategy 4 – Moving Average Trend Trading

The next strategy that a new trader can use is known as the moving average trend trading strategy. The moving averages are used as a way to help you pick out the right entry and exit points on whichever stocks you are trading. There are many stocks that will get on their morning trend and then will be either on the downside or upside trend. You would then be able to see their moving averages in the one and minute charts. This is beneficial to you as the trader because you are able to ride out whatever trend shows up by following these moving averages.

While this kind of strategy does sound a little complicated to work with, it is actually a simple one to choose. Some of the steps that you will want to use for the moving average trend strategy include:

- When you are looking at your graphs and checking out your stock in play, you should look to see if there is a trend that is forming near or at the moving average. When you see this, it is time for you to consider getting into the market with this strategy. You will need to also spend some time looking at the trading data from the day before. This helps you to get an idea of how the moving average has changed and how the stock is responding to this average.

- After you have looked over the charts and seen which moving average is the best for your trade, you can purchase the stock. If you would like, you can also wait a little longer and confirm the moving average is the support. Consider purchasing close to this moving average line, or as close as you can.

- Then you can pick out your stop points. You should have your stop about five to ten cents below the line for the moving average. If you are doing this with a candlestick chart, you must make sure that you have your start close to your moving average and then do a long position.

- After you enter the market, you will just ride out this trend until your moving average breaks.

It is important to remember that you should never use a trailing stop if you are working with the moving average trend strategy. This one is also one of those strategies where you must give it your full attention, or the market may get away from you. While the scanner can be nice for finding the right trades you want to use, make sure the scanner is turned off and your eyes are turned on when you are doing the trade.

If you see that your chosen stock is moving really high from the moving average, this means that you are making a great profit. At this time, it may be best to take the half position rather than going all the way to your break. This is going to make sure that you make some profit, and sometimes you will see the moving trend go down before the break. If you let this happen, it is possible to lose out on all of the profit. But with the half position, you can at least make some profit.

This is a strategy that some traders like to do but many beginners will avoid because it leaves you exposed to the market for a longer period of time. Some of these trending trades can last for a few hours or more, and for some day traders, this is just too long to trust the market. Most day traders like to go much faster, getting the profit in a few minutes, but if you are interested in trading over a few hours, it could be the best option for you.

Some beginners like this option because it helps them to get familiar with the trading and it does not require decision making that is quite as fast as the other options. You also will not have to rely on Hotkeys when starting. You can use the trending strategy to recognize your stop loss and your entry points easier than some of the other methods as well, something that is especially important for those traders who are stuck paying higher retail commissions and who are not able to get in and out of their trades without paying a big fee. Since the moving average trend strategy has an exit and entry point that are easy to see, it is easier to get a good profit with only two orders, which can save some traders money.

Chapter 11:
Day Trading Strategy 5 – Resistance Trading

Support and resistance trading are really popular and you will probably find a lot of traders who decide to go with this kind of strategy to help them do well. In these cases, support will be the price level when buying is so strong that it can reverse or interrupt the current downtrend that is going on. When your current downtrend ends up hitting a new support level, it will bounce. The support will then be shown on a chart using a horizontal line that will connect at least two bottoms.

On the other hand, the resistance will be the opposite. This is the price level where the selling position is so strong that it can reverse or interrupt the uptrend. When your uptrend hits that resistance level, the trend will stop and sometimes it will even tumble down. Resistance can be represented on your chart by a horizontal line that will connect at least two tops.

It is possible to get minor resistance or support. These will cause the trend to pause. But when you are working with a support or a resistance that is considered major, it can make the trend reverse. Traders who use this strategy will buy at the support and then sell at the resistance, often causing the strategy to be more effective because of the way they are behaving.

You will need to take a look at the daily charts to find the right resistance and support lines and sometimes it is difficult to find a line that is clear and easy to use. There are some days when you won't be able to make a line at all and you may need to choose a different strategy to work with for that day. If you can create that line, then this is a great strategy to work with.

There are some steps that you can use with the charts that you have available to help draw your own support and resistant lines. Some of the steps you can take to make this process easier and to really use this strategy include:

- Remember those indecision candles? You are going to see these in areas of support and resistance. These candles often show that buys and sellers are fighting with each other to see who has the most control over the price.

- Often half dollars and whole dollars can be good support and resistance levels. This is especially true when you work on stocks under $10. If you can't find your support or your resistance lines, check here and see if your line would work there.

- When you make your own lines, you need to have the most recent data available. This ensures that you are getting the best information for that stock.

- The more that your line is able to touch the extreme price of the stock, the better option this line is for your support and resistance. If it is too far from this extreme point, then it is not going to have enough value to make it strong.

- Only look at any support or resistance lines that stay with the current price range. For example, if the stock's price is around $20 right now, you do not need to look at the region on the graph where the stock randomly jumped up to $40.

This is not an area where the stock will probably go back to so it doesn't make much sense to work from there.

- Many times the support and resistance is not just one exact number. Often it is more of an area. If you come up with a support or resistance that is about $19.69 then you know that the movement is somewhere near that number, not exactly that number. You can usually estimate that the area is going to be somewhere between five to ten cents above or under that line.

- The price that you want to work from will need to have a clear bounce off that level. If you can't find that this price bounces at that level, then this is not a good support or resistance level for you to work with. Your levels need to be really easy to notice and need to make sense for the charts you look at. If you have any questions about whether you picked the right one or not, it's not the right one.

When we first create these lines, drawing them can be tricky. You want to make sure that you are getting the right support and resistance lines so that you know how to base your trades. But after you practice a bit, and test out your ideas with some backtesting, it will be easier to do and you can easily use this method with any trade that you want.

Once those lines have been drawn, you can then work on a good trading strategy to help you purchase and sell your chosen stocks based on these lines. Some of the best steps to help you with resistance trading include:

- Right when you wake up start to create your own watchlist. Look at the charts that you have available and then pick out the right support and resistance lines to go with that information.
- Set up the five-minute chart and watch the price action for a bit looking at your lines. If you find that near your lines there is an indecision candle forming, then this is confirmation that you picked a good area, and it is time to enter into the trade. Try to purchase the stock close to the support level to help reduce your risks.
- At this time, you also need to determine the right time to withdraw to make a profit if possible.

- Keep this trade open, even when you withdraw. This allows you to hit your target for profit, or until the stock gets to a new support or resistance level.
- Some traders decide that it is better to trade at half-positions that are near their profit target. Then they can move the stop up a bit to their entry point to get a breakeven point.
- If you look through your daily charts and there aren't any support or resistance levels that are obvious, you should close up the trade.

You will be surprised at how many of your trades can work with this method, and if it is done properly, it will alert you to the best time to enter and exit the market. You may need to practice creating these lines when you start, but after that, it gets easier and it will help you to make profitable trades.

Chapter 12:
Day Trading Strategy 6 – Opening Range Breakout

Now it is time to look at another popular trading strategy that you can work with, known as the opening range breakout. This strategy is a good one for beginners because it can signal a point for entry, but you will find it doesn't tell you where you should target your profit. You can pick out the profit you want to reach based on other strategies that are in this guidebook. The opening range breakout is just to be used as an entry signal, but if you use the rules for trading, then you need to come up with your own exit point as well.

To work with the opening range breakout, you should pay attention to what is going on in the market. When you look at the charts during this time, you will notice that the Stocks in Play go through a violent price action. Buyers and sellers are flooding the market right when it opens and the first five minutes can be a crazy time. New investors and traders will also choose to get into the market right when it opens for the day.

Some investors will look at this time and notice that their chosen position went down through the night. They may panic if they don't realize what is going on and sell off their stocks. There are plenty of new investors who come in and see that the stock is at a low price. They will jump onto that stock before the price of that stock goes back up. Both of these movements are important because they are going to determine the stock's price and where it will go during that day.

As a day investor who will not hold onto their position for more than a day, you will want to wait out the beginning of the markets open. Wait at least five minutes before you choose which stock to invest in. When all those sellers or buyers enter the market, it is hard to determine who is going to become the winner in the market. You don't want to guess wrong during this crazy time and it is best to wait at least a few minutes to make sure you can see the solid trends in the market before investing.

Once this opening period is over, the trader can work on the plan they want to use for trading. For this strategy, you want to do a plan that is based on either half an hour to an hour breakout. There are some that like to work with a smaller time frame such as fifteen minutes. The longer the time frame that you choose to work on with this strategy, the less volatility so often this is easier for a beginner to use.

Like with many of the other setups that we have talked about in this guidebook, the opening range breakout strategy is going to work the best with either mid-cap or large stocks or ones that won't go through huge and unpredictable price swings while you hold onto them. You also want to make sure that you don't go into this type of strategy with some low float stocks. Pick out a stock that has the ability to trade inside a range smaller than the ATR, or the Average True Range.

Working with the opening range breakout strategy, there are a few steps that you will need to follow. These steps include:

- After you have had some time to create your watchlist in the morning, you should wait until the stock market has time to settle down, so wait about five minutes. During this time, watch the price action and the opening range. You can also check out how many shares are traded during that time and then figure out from that information if the stock is going down or up. This time is when a ton of orders go through the market and you want to look at these numbers to see how liquid a stock actually is.

- During this time, you can also look through to see what the ATR of that stock is. You want the opening range to be smaller compared to the ATR so make sure the ATR number is nearby.

- Once those first five minutes of the market opening are finished, you may see that the stock will stay in that opening range a bit longer depending on what traders and investors want to do. However, if you see at this time that the stock is breaking out of this range, it is time to enter the trade. Enter the trade going the same direction of the breakout. If you can, go long if you see the breakout is going up, but go short if the breakout is going down.

- Pick out a good target for your profit as well. You can find this by looking at the daily levels from the previous day and identify where the stock is before the market opens. You can also look at the previous days' close, along with the moving averages, to come up with a good target.

- If you can't find the right technical level for your chosen target or for the exit, you can choose to go long and then look for signs of weakness. On the other hand, if you want to take a short position, and then the stock goes high, this shows you the stock is strong and you want to cover the position as much as you can.

This method is going to work when you are doing the opening range and can work with any time frame that you want such as fifteen minutes or half an hour, but the steps above are for a five-minute trade. You will have to watch the market and find out what is the best opening range breakout depending on the market you are working with.

The opening range breakout is one that works well and can help ensure that you won't be fooled by any changes that occur right when the market opens that morning. But you do get the option to use it to look at how the market is doing for the day. Just make sure that when you do the opening range breakout, you don't trade during the first five to ten minutes or you may be caught in the wrong side of things.

The beginning of the market can be really volatile and it just isn't a good idea to jump on during this time. But after the opening of the market is done, you will be able to move into the market and utilize the breakouts that occur after it is done.

Chapter 13:
Day Trading Strategy 7 –
Red to Green Trading

While all of the different strategies that we have talked about in this guidebook can be great options to help you do well with day trading, as long as you do them properly, another option that you can choose to work with is the red to green option. The red to green trading strategy is going to rely on information that you can gather from the close on the previous day to let you know where the stock is going to go today. You can then make informed decisions to help you trade in the market.

While you look at this historical information, look at the current price of the stock. If the current price of the stock is higher than what you say on the previous day, the market is moving up, going from a green day to a red day. This means that the percentage your price has changed is going to be negative. In most platforms, this negative number is going to be shown as red. This is known as a green to red move.

You can also see things go the other way as well. If you see that the price of the stock is lower than what is on the graphs on the previous day, this shows how the market is moving from a red day over to a green day. This means that the price change percentage is going to be positive for this trade. This positive change is going to be shown as green on most of the platforms that you use. This is an example of a red to green move.

The strategy that you use for this one is going to be the same whether you are moving from green to red or from red to green, except for the direction that your trade is going in, or whether you are doing a short position or a long position for it. To keep things simple for this strategy, we are going to stick with one of these and you can just follow the same rules depending on which type of market you are moving in.

We are going to start with the red to green strategy. To do this kind of trading strategy, you will need to follow these steps:

- When you start out the day and you are creating a new watchlist, you will need to pull up information about the previous day. Look specifically at the close checking out what the price action was at that time.

- If you see these charts and notice that the stock is moving to where it was the previous day at the close with a high volume, you will want to go along with this strategy. You will want to use the profit target that occurred on the close of the previous day.

- The stop loss that you are going to use for the red to green strategy should be as near your technical level as possible. This means that if you purchase near the VWAP, the stop loss needs to end up where the VWAP has a break. If you want to purchase near a support level or the moving average, then you can place the stop loss either near that moving average or near the break in your chosen support level.

- It is a good idea to sell at the profit target. If the price ends up moving in your favor, it is time to consider bringing the stop loss up the breakeven point and then make sure to not let this price go against you. When you are done with that, the red to green move should start working right away.

You will be able to use an approach in a similar way if you want to work on the green to red strategy because they work pretty much the same way.

Chapter 14:

Day Trading Strategy 8 – Working with Either a Fundamental Analysis or a Technical Analysis to Form the Basis of Your Trades

Two of the basic strategy ideas that are found in many forms of stock market investing are fundamental analysis and technical analysis. In fact, many of the strategies that we have already talked about in this guidebook have touched on these two important topics especially the technical analysis. But how can you use these ideas to help you pick out the right stocks to purchase and make a profit from in day trading? This chapter is going to spend some time looking at the differences in a fundamental analysis and a technical analysis and the benefits of using each one.

How to Use Fundamental Analysis in Your Day Trading Activities

The fundamental analysis is a bit different compared to what to some of the other strategies that we find in this guidebook. While most of the other strategies ask you to take a look at the graphs around a stock and then determine when you want to invest and when you want to get out of the market, the fundamental analysis is going to look more at the company that is behind the stock, and how that company is doing.

The fundamental analysis is often going to look at a variety of factors behind the stock and factors that may not influence the price right now but could in the future. It looks to see who is running the business, what changes they are planning to make in the future if there is any change in the management, the debt to profit ratio of the company and more. It basically looks to see how financially secure the company is, something that isn't necessarily going to show up in the stock charts you look at.

Often, this fundamental analysis is going to be saved for long-term investing, something that you don't see much with day traders. It takes into account how the price of the company will go into the future when compared to where it is now, but these changes are often going to occur over weeks, months, or even years. Day trading takes place in one day. Because of this, most day traders will not use this information to help them make decisions about which stocks to trade in.

As a day trader, you probably won't spend a lot of time working on fundamental research. You could probably guess this by all the other strategies that we have in this book. Sure, most traders know that a demand in ethanol is going to make a difference in the price of corn during a particular time period. But day traders want to focus more on what the price is going to do right now compared to where it was a few minutes ago.

They aren't really that interested in what the price will do past that time period. How a farm bill, if it is passed, will affect the price of ethanol in the future is not really something that a day trader cares that much about.

However, having some knowledge about the fundamentals of a particular stock, or the basic factors that are going to affect how the supply and the demand of a security are going to do in all markets, can really help a day trader respond to various news events that they hear in the day. In addition, some day traders choose to switch their strategy a bit on occasion and go over to the swing trading strategy because they find that it will provide them more profits during that particular trade.

But knowing too much information about a company can be a challenge when it comes to a day trader. They don't need to know who runs the company, about big management changes, how the finances are doing, or any of that. In fact, many day traders can enter and exit the market without finding out about any of this information at all. Outside of little news releases and how that information will affect the stock and the market over the next few hours, they don't need the fundamental analysis that much, which is why you won't see it much in the day trading strategies.

Knowing a little bit about the fundamentals about a company can help in some cases but often it can slow down your day trading process. If you plan to trade daily in one or two particular stocks because they seem to follow the strategy you are going with, take some time to learn a few of these fundamentals. This will help you to notice when trends are changing and can keep you on the lookout for any big news events that can get you ahead of the game. Otherwise, it is probably not really worth your time to look at the fundamental analysis as a day trader.

Working with the Technical Analysis as a Day Trader

The technical analysis is going to work slightly different than what you find with the fundamental analysis. The fundamental analysis is going to look at the financial statements and more of a company to determine what the fair value of the business is, compared to what it is selling for on the stock market. With a technical analysis, the trader is going to assume that the price of the company's stock is already reflecting its value and then will keep its focus on statistical analysis of price movements.

A technical analysis is sometimes seen as complicated, but it basically has you look at graphs and determine the best time to enter into the market with your day trading. You can look at a lot of the different strategies that we showed in this guidebook and see a lot of options on how to do a technical analysis.

The technical analysis is going to be a method of evaluating stocks. It is going to use a statistical analysis of the activity in the market such as volume and price. The trader who uses this is not going to attempt to measure the intrinsic value of a security. Instead, they will use a variety of tools and other charts in order to find patterns they can use for their own investment decisions. There are actually quite a few different types of technical analysis. Some are going to rely on patterns that are found in a chart, others are going to use technical oscillators and indicators. Most traders are going to use some combination of these techniques. In any case, you would use historical price and volume data to help make decisions which are not seen with a fundamental analysis.

There are three assumptions that come with a technical analysis. These assumptions include:

- History is often going to repeat itself.
- The price tends to move in a trend.
- The market is going to discount everything.

Before we move on here, realize there are a lot of different options when you do a technical analysis. You can get things like chart patterns or a statistical indicator. With all of the strategies that we talked about earlier, you can look and see that a technical analysis takes many different forms.

The Market Is Going to Discount out Everything

Many experts are going to criticize this kind of analysis because it is only going to consider the movements in price while completely ignoring all of the fundamental factors that should be behind these decisions. But if you are a day trader who just wants to take advantage of some of the price movements that happen in the market, then this is not a bad thing.

As a technical analyst, you go into the market believing that everything from the fundamentals of a company to broad market factors and even the market psychology of the company is already going to be shown in the price of the stock. This is an important factor because it explains why a technical analyst is not going to concern themselves with the fundamental factors before they make decisions for investing. They assume that it is all tied together and then reflected in the price that the charts show.

Since all of this information is shown inside the current market price of the security, the only thing that is left for a trader is to analyze the price movements. These movements are not so much related to the company at that time but more related to the supply and the demand for that stock in the market at that time. If the day trader can estimate the supply and demand right at certain points during the day, they can translate that into some good profits.

Prices Tend to Move in a Trend

As a technical analysis, you are going to learn that the price for a stock is going to move in some kind of trend. This is sometimes a short-term, mid-term, or long-term trend. This means that the price of a stock is more likely to continue a past trend rather than move around erratically. It will only get off this trend if some big even happens that pushes it there which is why many day traders keep an eye on the news during their trades. Most technical trading strategies are based on the assumption that the price will move in a trend.

History Is Often Going to Repeat Itself

Those who decide to work with the technical analysis are going to believe that history will repeat itself even when it comes to the stock market. The repetitive nature of these movements in price will be attributed to market psychology. These trends are very predictable and can be followed, and they will be based on the emotions of other traders, including emotions like excitement or fear.

A technical analysis is going to use some chart patterns to help them predict and analyze these emotions, as well as the movements in the market that come from these emotions, in order to understand the trends seen on the chart. While there are many forms of this technical analysis that have been used for more than 100 years, they are relevant because they show how these patterns in price movements will repeat themselves over and over again.

If you believe that the movement of price is going to keep up with the same trends that it did throughout history, then you can use this information to help you make informed decisions to help you reach the right investment options. This may take a little bit of time to accomplish, but with some research and some notes, you can use that same information to help you make smart decisions for your investments for a long time to come.

The Bottom Line

As an investor, you can easily work with either of these types of analysis. But while long-term investments can come up with some options that work great under either of these options, most day traders will just stick with the technical analysis, mainly because they don't care about the long-term implications of the stock and the information from this analysis is enough for their type of trading. Most of the strategies that come with day trading will rely on these technical analyses, and you basically just look at the charts surrounding the stock and make informed decisions based on that information. There are different ways to do this, you simply need to explore some of the other day trading strategies and pick the one that works best for you.

Chapter 15:
Other Strategies to
Consider with Day Trading

The other strategies that we have talked about for day trading are great options for a beginner. And many times, there will be one of the strategies that you choose to go with. As long as you use the strategy in the proper manner, and you stick with it for you're the entirety of your trade, you can see success with it. However, you may find that you don't like one option or the market is not doing what you want, so you are ready to change things up a little bit. Let's take some time to look at some of the other strategies that you can consider when you want to get into day trading.

Gap Up, Inside Bar, Breakout Strategy

The first strategy we are going to work on is the gap up, inside the bar, breakout strategy. This trading signal is going to start when you look at some of your charts and you see there is a gap up. Then, if the second or the third ten-minute bar develops and it becomes an inside bar, then this is the perfect setup that you need to make this strategy work for you.

Some traders will do this option but change it up a bit. They will work with some stocks that have a partial gap up, rather than the full gap. But traders only want to do this if they are listed high on the gainer's list. When we are looking for this partial gap, rather than a full gap we are talking about our setup having a gap that is higher than were it ended up at the previous days close. In addition, this gap still needs to come in lower than the previous days' high. This can provide you with some good signals that the stock is the right one but it ensures that you have more options to work with from the beginning compared to working with the full gap.

When you are working with this strategy, you want to keep the charts to a minimum time frame. For example, you may only want to go with one or two of these ten-minute bars before you start with your inside bar. Beware though, if you see that there are more than these two ten-minute bars, it means that the price has had way too much movement at this point and you should avoid this option because it isn't the most effective setup.

As soon as you have the right inside bar, without too much volatility going on in the market, it is time to purchase your stop. Make sure that this stop is right about the high you see in your bar. The trigger is the breakout that is above your inside bar.

At this point, you may have to wait for a little bit. You want to find the right trade signal that will make you go long. Then, if you have already put the right stop in place, it is time for you to think about some logistics such as where and when you want to exit this trade. You need to put the stop in the right place because if it is hit, you will want to cut your losses and get out of the market before trying out some new trade.

Gap Up, Attempt to Fill, Breakout

We can also use the gap up idea to work on the next strategy. This one is pretty simple to work with and it can rely on the common sense of the trader to make it work. As the name sounds, you will look for a stock that has a new gap up, and that is then trying to get this gap filled. Whether the stock is actually able to fill up this gap to the previous days high or not isn't going to be as important with this strategy. The important thing with this particular strategy is that the market needs to look like it is trying to fill up that gap. Even if it doesn't succeed, it should at least try, or this is not the right stock.

For this process to work, you must look at the chart and see that the price dips down below the first ten-minute bar you set. You do not want to see the first bar being the one that fills in the gap, or you can't use this method and see success. A small and gradual attempt to fill this gap after the first bar can work because it shows that the price will head in the right direction, but it won't do it too quickly.

When you see that after these few steps the stock starts to gap up a bit and then the market continues to try and close that gap, it means that you will be able to find quite a few traders who are trading short. And these traders will look at the market and assume that the stock is going to finish its downward trend. They will either sell off to not lose money, or they will trade with the assumption that the stock goes down.

When the stock does turn around and with the pattern we are looking at, it will go back up and these traders will be in a bad position. They may have lost any gains that they earned in the process and they will need to decide whether the stop they picked out, in the beginning, can actually make them some money or not.

From here, the pattern is going to continue and you will notice the breakout. This breakout is going to be very fast paced and it can occur at a volume that is higher than normal. The traders that went short in this situation will feel squeezed without the stop. Some of these traders will decide that it is best to get back into the market here using the long position instead of the short position.

This helps to increase the breakout even more than before. You can get in on the low part of the trend, when the price of the stocks is lower, and then sell once that breakout occurs and everyone is trying to get back in. If you can read the charts and know that the trend is not going to continue down but will end with a breakout that goes upwards, you can get on at the right time and see some profits in the process.

The Gap Up, Afternoon Breakout (Also Known as the Gainer)

Depending on the market you enter when you are ready to trade, another simple option that you can choose for your trading is known as the gap up, afternoon breakout. Just like with the other few strategies that we have discussed in this guidebook, you are going to use your scanner to help you find the gap. The difference here is that you are not going to do this right when the market opens, like what you would do with the other options. Instead, you are going to search around for these gaps in the late morning or early in the afternoon.

During your scan for this one, you want to search around for some simple patterns. In specific, you want to look for consolidating and basing patterns. You want to look at the charts and see that there is a big and strong rise in the price that occurred throughout the whole morning. Then, you want to look at the later morning, or even in the early afternoon, and see that the price has settled down a bit to be less volatile than before.

Often when you are looking at the stocks that did well in the morning with their performance because they have a higher than average volume are the ones that will often make a high that is a bit more than average. Then these stocks are going to settle down a bit and relax. At the time period when you should trade, these stocks will look pretty steady and like they aren't heading up or down. If you see this, then you know that is the stock you want to trade here. Once you see that stock inching back up to its resistance point, then it is time to put in a buy stop order and then wait for the breakout that will come soon.

While this is a simple method to work with and can be a great way for a beginner to start, there are a few drawbacks with it because there are a few stocks that won't be able to make it to the right starting points. You can always leave the stock and take the loss if it doesn't move. But there are some stocks that will do really well with this and will explode quickly. If you jump on at the right time, you can make a ton of money with this.

The Fibonacci Retracement Pattern

Some of the other strategies that we have discussed in this chapter are a bit shorter in time frame compared to some of the others. This one is going to be used on a thirty-minute chart. On this chart, you want to look for a stock that reached higher highs compared to what it did on the two days before. You want to have a 15 SMA cross above the 35 SMA on that day. The main thing that you want to look for when using this idea is to find a price that can give you a retracement back to both the 28 and the 68 percent the next morning. You will see that this happens when you look through your 30-minute chart and you see that there is either an inverted M or U pattern.

Once you see that this price is moving back over to the retracement level on the following morning, then you can look to see that the price is forming on a rising bar looking at the MACD histogram. Remember that you do not need to get the numbers at perfect levels but you will need to stay near that 62 and 38 percent as much as possible. The main thing here is that you want to see a good retracement with the movement back to where that first impulse showed up. Once you are able to find this setup on the chart, you will notice that it is time to see a breakout trigger on the ten-minute chart.

Once you see that this happens, you need to switch over and start looking at the ten-minute chart. This chart is going to show you the right information. You will wait for the breakout of the high that was on your thirty-minute bar. When you see this happen, enter into the market and then you can wait for that breakout to occur so you can make a profit.

Gap Down, Fill Gap, Inside Bar, Breakout

There are some traders who feel that it is a bad idea for you to enter the market with a stock that is gapped down. If you look at the stock and see that it meets some other criteria, you can find that a short squeeze action is the best way to help send these stocks up for that day which will result in you earning a profit as well.

This is an easier option that you may think in the beginning. You will need to use some of the ten-minute charts in the beginning. If you are looking at these charts and notice that there is a down gap that is filling up, and then there are some second and third ten-minute bars that form as the inside bar, then you are int e perfect setup to make this strategy work.

When you see this happen, you will need to place the buy stop above the high for this new inside bar. The trigger that will tell you to make a purchase is when you see that a breakout is going to occur above the high for that bar that is on the inside. You can then place the stop order so that it is low of the inside bar. You can also choose to do another area if you find that it is lower than the bar to increase your profits.

Other Methods That Can Help with Day Trading for a Beginner

This guidebook has spent some time talking about the different day trading strategies that you can use when it comes to doing this trading strategy. All of these have provided professional traders with success and some good profits, but you need to know which one to use and work on learning exactly how to do it. If you know how to use the strategy properly and you learn how to keep with it throughout the whole trade, then you can make any of them work for you.

There are also a few other popular trading strategies that you can work with that will make it easier for you to earn money in the stock market with day trading. Some of the best trading strategies that you can use and that work well for a beginner include:

- News trading.

  News trading is a great option to go with because you will listen for some big news events and watch out for new trends that can form before others find out about them. If you know that a company is about to release a big announcement soon, you can easily get onto the stock, purchase it when the price is low, and later that day, when the announcement is out, you can sell the stock for a higher price when everyone else jumps on. You need to be able to read hints in the market to make this work. If you jump on after the news is released, you will be too late and won't make much of a profit.

- Range trading.

  This is a good strategy to use for those traders who have a lot of time and patience to help them get the right research done. With this trading strategy, you may need to spend some time following a stock, learning the range for lows and highs for that stock throughout time. You can then pick out the best time to trade based on these highs and lows.

- Pairs trading.

  For this one to work, you need to make sure that you are trading in pairs. You want to first work on picking a category that you want to trade in and then you will go short on the stock that you see as well. You would do the second trade as well, going long on a trade that you consider strong. When you do these two trades at the same time, it is much easier for you to make some profits in the process.

- Contrarian trading.

  We spent some time earlier in this guidebook talking about one of the strategies where you are going to follow the actions that the market is taking. If you see that the overall market is going up, you would make a purchase. But if you see that the market is going down, you would sell the stocks. This strategy is going to work a bit different. You will look at the trends that come with the market and then trade against them. When you see that the market is starting to go up, you sell the stock. And when the market is heading down, you will make a purchase. This can be hard to work with as a day trader because it is the opposite of what they are used to working with. But if you do it properly, it can be a good way to make money.

- Chart patterns.

  The chart pattern is a great option to work with when you are trying to earn profits in day trading. It often helps out when finding the right entry and exit points on an investment. If you use these charts and use some technical indicators such as the relative strength index, the rate of change, or the commodity channel index, you will be able to figure out the best times to enter and exit a trade. You can pick out the chart pattern that makes the most sense for you. Just put the right information into your chart and then make decisions from there.

- Technical indicators.

  If you like to have a lot of information before you make your decisions with day trading, then technical indicators will be the best option for you. These technical indicators will be important to the day traders because they can help show trends in the market that may be hard to see on their own. Looking at these indicators and making sure that you can interpret them the proper way will ensure that you can make a profit.

As you can see, there are a lot of different trading strategies. Many traders have worked over the years to create strategies that can help them to earn a profit with their stocks, and with all of the different types of stocks that are available, you are sure to find one that will work with the strategy that you would prefer. As a beginner, it is up to you to learn some more about these strategies and then pick out the one that you would like to use. With the right strategy and the right stock, you will be able to earn a good profit in no time with day trading.

Chapter 16:
Steps to Complete a
Successful Trade

Now that this guidebook has taken some time to discuss a lot of the great trading strategies that you can use to see success with day trading, we are going to put it all together to help you come up with the steps you need to take to really get your trade off the ground. You will have to do a bit of the work here such as setting up the account and picking out the strategy that you want to work with but this chapter can be your checklist to help you out when you are ready to perform the actual trade. Let's take a look at the steps that you should take in order to do a successful trade in day trading.

Building up Your Watch List

The first step when you are ready to get started in day trading is to do some research. When you first wake up in the morning, look over your notes and your research and then use that information to create a good watchlist. This watchlist can be important because it can limit you down to just a few options that you plan to use for trading on that day. There are thousands of stocks on the market and making this watchlist will make it so much easier for you to pick the right stocks to invest in.

There are different methods you can use to create this watchlist. But one of the best options is to use a scanner. These scanners can look for specific criteria that you want out of a stock and can make things faster than trying to look through them all on your own. To make the scanner work, you just need to list out the requirements that you want the stock to meet and then the scanner will alert you as soon as it finds one that meets these.

You do need to take this a step further. When you see a few stocks show up on the scanner, make sure to check them out personally rather than just investing in the first ones that show up. When you look through the results on the scanner, you will quickly see that a few are worth your time and you may invest in them, but there will be plenty that is not worth your time and you can skip over these.

Decide Which of These Stocks Work Best for You

After the scanner has given you a few options for stocks that meet your requirements, you can decide which of these are the best stocks. You may have a specific strategy that you would like to go with and then choose the stock that seems to be following that strategy the best. You can always change strategies from one day to the next, or you can choose to stick with one strategy if it is serving your purpose.

As we discussed in some of our strategies before, make sure that you do not trade in the market for at least the first five minutes after the market opens. Some professionals wait even longer than these five minutes for the market to settle down.

There can be a ton of commotion and crazy ups and downs in the market during those first few minutes

and investing at this time can hurt your profits. If you spend time looking at your scanner and then investigating the stocks that you receive, it will probably be at least five or more minutes before you are ready to enter the market anyway, but it is still important to be aware of this volatility and learn how to avoid it.

Put That Entry and Exit Strategy in Place

Now that you have a few stocks that are ready to go, you're probably excited to get into the market and start doing your trading. Before you make that purchase, you need to finish up your strategies. This isn't just the overall strategy but also the enter and the exit strategy so you know how to get into and out of the market at the right times.

The first strategy you should work with here is your entry strategy. This is the place where you are comfortable and will purchase your stock. Your aim is to get this entry point as low as you can so that you don't spend too much money and to increase your profits later on. When you look through the charts for that stock, you should be able to figure out a safe entry point that will provide you with a reasonable price on that stock.

You also need to come up with an exit strategy. It is important to have a stop for losing money and one for earning money. First, let's look at the stop for losing money. There are times when the strategies that you pick or the decisions that you make are not going to turn out how you wanted and the stock may start to lose money. The point of this stop is to ensure that you can control how much money you will lose in the process. Once the stock ends up reaching this number, you will withdraw from the market, no matter what the stock does later on.

Without this stop, you could end up with a little bit of trouble. Many new traders see that the stock is going down, and they keep riding it out. They hope that the market will turn around. Sometimes the market will turn around, but then there are times when the market will stay low or keep going down. And without a stop, you could be without a whole bunch of money. Depending on how far the market goes, you may not be able to cover the losses either. It is much better to have that stop in place and then exit the market at a comfortable loss rather than letting things get out of hand. You can always get back into the market later on if things begin to improve.

After you pick out the stop loss, it is time to get your profit stop in place. This is one that a lot of beginners are going to skip because they assume that it is best to just ride out the market until they stop making profits. But day trading finds that the market is going to do a lot of ups and downs, even in markets that are pretty stable. You want to have a profit stop so that you can get out of the market before the prices go down and you are not able to earn any profits at all. Yes, it's possible that the market will have a big breakout and you are going to miss out on some potential profits, but it's just as possible that the market could tank as well and you would lose your profits.

Purchase the Stocks You Want

After you created your watchlist and came up with your enter and exit strategies to keep you safe, it is time to actually go into the market and make your purchase. You will want to have all the criteria in place for that stock before doing this. But if you are working with a strategy, that is going to outline the criteria for you, so just follow that.

If you plan to work with your broker when doing day trading, you would just give them your order to get the trade started. The order is going to include a ton of information that can help the broker do everything that you want. This would include information on which stocks, in particular, you want to purchase, how many shares of each you want to purchase, how much you will spend on these stocks, when you want to enter the market, and when you want to exit the market. The broker is then able to take that information and place the order for you in the system.

There is also the option for you to do all of the work on your own. This is fine to do but most beginner traders are not going to pick this option because they worry about messing things up or doing something wrong. Make sure that if you are doing this choice that you work with a good platform that can get the work done quickly for you. If the platform ends up being really slow, or there are some mistakes done on your side, it could really ruin your trade.

Pay Attention to the Market Until the Trade Is Closed

You will quickly find that day trading has some differences compared to other stock trading options. Many other options are longer-term; you purchase the stock and then ride out the market, hoping that your choice will go up over some time. But with day trading, you are only letting the trade occur in one day. The purchase of the stock, as well as the sale of it, all need to happen sometime between open and close of the same day.

This does make day trading a riskier option to work with compared to some of the other stock trading options. This means that you need to really want the market and make some quick decisions on when to buy and sell your stocks. If you don't watch the market, then how are you going to be able to make these quick changes when needed?

Day trading is unique as it takes advantage of the little ups and downs in the value of a stock during the day. If you look at the long-term charts of a stock, you will notice that it stays pretty steady. There may have been a few news announcements or a few other things that come up on the charts that change the trend, but overall, the stock will probably go upwards. But if you look at a week or even a day of historical value on the stock, you will see a lot of little ups and downs. None of them are that big, but they are there. Day trading is attempting to capitalize on these.

As a day trader, you get to focus on watching these ups and downs that occur during the day. This can make it easier to know when you should purchase a stock in the first place and then it helps you to figure out when you can sell the stocks to make the biggest profits, or to keep your losses to a minimum.

Once you enter into a trade, you need to pay attention to the market and there may be times when the market changes quickly and you will need to make some quick changes to your position, or close it out, to help you earn more profits or keep the losses down as much as possible. Day trading is not one of those methods where you can place the order and then walk away. If you don't have the time to sit and closely watch the market, make sure to not place an order until you have more time.

Sell Your Stocks When They Reach Your Original Exit Points

Remember how we sent some exit strategies earlier? This is when they are going to come into play. These numbers are important to the day trading because they take some of the risks that come with day trading and will limit how much money you will lose if the market doesn't go the way you would like to. Regardless of how the market goes, you want to stick with your exit and entry points. The second you ignore them, you have let the emotions play into the mix, and you are not going to win as much as you think.

It is a good idea to listen to your exit point not only when the market is going down but also when the market is going up. Some people understand why they should follow the exit strategy when the market is going down and they do not want to end up losing too much money in the market. It is a bit harder on them when the market is going up. They may have placed a stop for how much profit they wanted to make, but then they see the market still goes up and they do not want to get out at that time.

While it may be hard, make sure that you are listening to your exit strategy, even when the market is going up. Sure, the market may go past that point, but then it may hit a sharp downturn and you could lose all of that profit. This is another method in place to ensure that your investment stays safe. If the market continues to do well and keeps going up, you will be able to jump back in later on.

Take Some Time to Reflect on That Trade and Write Down Some of the Information as Research Later

As a beginner in the day trading world, there are a lot of things to learn about the market. This is even truer if you have never invested in the past. As a trader, it is your job to learn as you go and make some changes if it is needed. But when you are learning a lot of strategies and keeping track of a large number of trades that are done in day trading, it can be hard to remember everything over time.

Getting a journal and writing down some of your mistakes, your tips, and more after each trade can make a difference. You don't have to write down a lot of information unless you want to. Just have a few lines or a paragraph. This may seem like it wastes your time. But if you ever get stuck on a trade later on, or if you are trying to figure out why you are in a slump and not getting the profits that you want, looking back through this information can make a big difference in how things go in the future.

Startup Your Second (And Third and Fourth and So on) Trade

Day trading moves very fast. It is likely that your first trade can be done in a few minutes, though as a beginner it will probably take a little bit longer to finish. If there is still time left in the day when you finish up that first trade, then go through these steps again and complete the next trade. Day traders earn a big profit simply by doing a bunch of little trades.

The more of these successful trades that you can get into one day, the more profit you will make. Just make sure that you are following the same steps that we talked about above and take the same precautions that you did with your first trade. If there is not enough time during the day, or you worry that you will rush yourself if you try to do another trade, it is fine to take a break and resume the next day.

There are times when you are going to get into the day trading market and you will make a bad trade in the morning. It may not have gone your way, you may have tried to switch your strategy part way through, or maybe you let your emotions get in the way. If the trade was really bad and you feel upset about it, then it is best to just call it good and take a step away from the market for the rest of the day.

As a beginner, this is especially important as you get your bearings. These losses can hurt a professional investor, much less a beginner, and if you stay in, you may resort to revenge trading, which basically leads to a downward spiral that can cost you way more money than just taking a break. Yes, you may want to earn more profit or get more experience in the market. But taking a break can give you time to get your head back in the game and will give you the renewed confidence to do better in the morning.

Getting started with your day trading adventure can be an exciting time. As long as you follow the rules, learn to read the market and you pick out a good strategy, you can make money with this investment choice! It is hard and very fast paced, but it is also a very rewarding form of investing that many people enjoy working with.

Conclusion

Thank you for making it through to the end of *Day Trading*. Let's hope it was informative and able to provide you with all of the tools you need to achieve your goals whatever they may be.

The next step is to take a look at the market at the time you read this guidebook and decide the best strategy to use. There are a lot of different strategies that you can work with, whether you are a beginner in day trading or not and the one that you choose can often help you pick out which stocks you want to invest in, as well as the enter and exit points of your trade. This guidebook will provide you with the information that you need to start out in day trading and make a profit, even as a beginner.

There are many traders, especially those who are beginners, who worry about getting started in day trading. They think that this is a dangerous or risky method of trading and they may choose to go with something else. But for those who truly know how to read the market, and who are willing to choose the right strategy and stick with it, day trading can be a great way to enter the market and make some good profits in the process. This guidebook will give you the tools and information that you need to be successful as a beginner in day trading.

Whether you are just getting started exploring some of your investment options in the stock market, or you are seriously considering day trading as your chosen investment vehicle, take some time to read through this guidebook to learn more about day trading and how it can work for you.

Finally, if you found this book useful in any way, a review on Amazon is always appreciated!